C000265104

Misc

Missing the Point?

*Finding our place in
the turning points of history*

Vaughan Roberts

Series Editor Jonathan Carswell

Authentic

LONDON ● COLORADO SPRINGS ● HYDERABAD

Copyright © 2007 Vaughan Roberts

13 12 11 10 09 08 07   7 6 5 4 3 2 1

First published 2007 by Authentic Media
9 Holdom Avenue, Bletchley, Milton Keynes, Bucks, MK1 1QR, UK
1820 Jet Stream Drive, Colorado Springs, CO 80921, USA
OM Authentic Media, Medchal Road, Jeedimetla Village,
Secunderabad 500 055, A.P., India
www.authenticmedia.co.uk
Authentic Media is a division of IBS-STL U.K., limited by guarantee,
with its Registered Office at Kingstown Broadway, Carlisle, Cumbria
CA3 0HA. Registered in England & Wales No. 1216232.
Registered charity 270162

The right of Vaughan Roberts to be identified as the Author of this Work
has been asserted by him in accordance with the Copyright, Designs
and Patents Act 1988

British Library Cataloguing in Publication Data
A catalogue record for this book is available from the British Library

ISBN-13: 978-1-85078-763-1
ISBN-10: 1-85078-763-8

Unless otherwise stated, Scripture quotations are taken from the HOLY
BIBLE, NEW INTERNATIONAL VERSION. Copyright © 1973, 1978,
1984 by the International Bible Society. Used by permission of Hodder
& Stoughton Limited. All rights reserved. 'NIV' is a registered trademark
of the International Bible Society UK trademark number 1448790

Cover Design by David McNeill
Print Management by Adare Carwin
Printed and bound in Great Britain by J.H. Haynes & Co., Sparkford

Introduction to the Exploring Christianity series

Rubbernecking. We've all done it, haven't we? Curiously having a nosey at something . . . keen to find out what's going on. Whether it's on the motorway with an accident on the other side, across a crowded street in town or as a man is arrested for shoplifting. Or perhaps an elderly lady has fainted and is treated by paramedics. There is just something about finding out what all the fuss is about.

Perhaps that's why you've picked up this book. Christianity and the person of Jesus might be something you know very little about, but you've heard or seen something that makes you want to know more and so here you are . . .

This is just one of a series of short books written for people who are just starting to look at what Christianity is all about. We hope that through this series you'll be able to explore a little more and find out the facts for yourself.

So, your invite is here . . . come rubberneck with us as we look at the issue of who Jesus is and find the answer to 'Is He relevant today?'

Jonathan Carswell
Series Editor

Notes about Bible references

If you have never read the Bible, or even looked through it, it can be quite confusing and daunting. It really doesn't need to be though.

There are 66 books that make up the Bible. The Bible is divided into two sections known as the Old Testament and the New Testament. The first four books of the New Testament, namely Matthew, Mark, Luke and John, are collectively known as the Gospels.

Throughout this *Exploring Christianity* series the Bible is mentioned either through the author's own paraphrase or through a direct quotation. When used, a footnote gives reference to where it can be found in the Bible.

For example, a footnote saying Romans 3:23 means that the quotation is taken from the book of Romans. Each book in the Bible is divided into chapters and these are numbered. This is what the first number stands for. Then, each chapter is broken up into verses. These are also numbered. In the example above this is what is the number 23 refers to. So if Romans 3:23 is referred to this means that you can read the quotation in the Bible by turning to the book of Romans, chapter 3, and looking at verse 23.

Introduction

> Is there a meaning to life? Where are we going? What is the purpose of it all? Is human history a random process going nowhere? Or is it under control – heading towards a goal, a destination? And what about my life? How does it fit into the bigger picture? Does it have a point?

Christians believe that the answers to all these questions are found in the Bible. It is an ancient book, written many centuries ago, but it is also God's message to us today; a message that focuses on one man, Jesus of Nazareth. His massive impact on both individuals and civilizations over the centuries is not in doubt. He never wrote a book, but He is the hero of history's number one bestseller. He never travelled out of His own country, but has more followers worldwide than any other person, alive or dead. He was born in an obscure Palestinian village and died in His early thirties. The world has never been the same since. One writer has said of Him: *'All the armies that ever marched, and all the navies that ever sailed, and all the parliaments that ever sat, and all the kings that ever reigned, put together, have not affected the life of man upon earth as has that one solitary life.'*

Jesus lived and died two thousand years ago, but millions in our world still worship Him as God and follow Him as their master. What do you make of Him? Could it be that this extraordinary man belongs not just to the past, but to the present and the future as well? Could He be the centre of history, as the Bible claims; the one who makes sense of life?

In this short booklet we will be looking at the most important turning points of history as outlined in the Bible. You might want to read this for yourself; although originally written in Hebrew and Greek it has been translated into most languages spoken today. Because it is a long book, I have tried to provide a brief summary that will help you understand what it is teaching – from creation to the end of the world in a few pages. We will discover what the Bible says about where we have come from and where we are going. That will help us to see what life is all about. It will leave us with a choice: will we fit in with God's plan for our lives or will we go our own way? I began to follow Christ at the age of eighteen. My life was turned upside-down and I have never regretted it since.

I began to follow Christ at the age of eighteen. My life was turned upside-down and I have never regretted it since.

In the beginning

The Bible opens with these dramatic words: *'In the beginning God created the heavens and the earth.'*[1] There was a time when God alone existed. Then He just said the word and the whole universe came into being. He had no materials to work with; He made everything out of nothing.

Scientists offer all sorts of theories about how life developed on earth, but they say very little about how that life came into being in the first place. There are two alternatives: either life began by chance or we were created.

Imagine that you go for a walk one day and come across a piece of wood in the exact shape of a bird. The beak, eyes, legs, and wings are all there in tiny detail. The possibility of such a precise likeness being produced by chance is so small that you would surely think the bird had been made by a skilful craftsman.

Doesn't the amazing world we live in force us to the same conclusion about its origin? Look up at the stars or at a view from a mountain peak. Is everything you see just an accident of nature?

And what about the complexity of it all? A television camera has 60,000 photo-electric elements which enable it, in a limited sense, 'to see'. Now compare this to the human eye. The eye – which focuses automatically, sees in all

[1] Genesis 1:1

weathers, and normally functions unceasingly for seventy or more years – contains more than 137 million elements. No wonder that Charles Darwin, who first described the theory of evolution, said that he could not believe with his mind that everything was created by chance.

We did not come into existence by accident: God had a purpose in mind. The book of Genesis reveals the Creator's plan. He made us *in his own image*.[2] It is true that we are part of the animal kingdom; but that is not all that we are – we are not just 'naked apes'. God has set us above the rest of His creation as those who uniquely reflect His character. Out of all that God has made, we alone are able to relate to Him. **That was His original plan for our lives: that we might live in His world in a perfect, loving relationship with Him.**

The description of Adam and Eve in the Garden of Eden presents a picture of human life as it was supposed to be. We are told that *'God saw all that he had made, and it was very good.'*[3] Human beings consciously submitted to God as their Creator and enjoyed the perfect life as a result: peace with God leading to peace with each other and with the world around them.

But things are very different now. Something has gone wrong and we no longer enjoy the friendship with God for which we were made – no wonder we feel empty sometimes. **There is something missing in our lives –**

only God can make us whole again. The Bible tells the story of how God, in His amazing love, planned to put things right and bring us back into friendship with Himself through His son Jesus. We will look at that plan in the next few pages, but first we must consider what went wrong with the perfect world God made.

Where it all went wrong

We live in a wonderful world that a loving God has made. And yet alongside all the beauty – all that is good – there is much that is very bad. The last century produced astonishing advances in our knowledge and capabilities: who in 1900 would have thought that by the dawn of the next millennium we would have landed on the moon, transplanted hearts, and broadcasted the same event simultaneously to millions of people on every continent? But can we really speak of progress?

When a survey invited people to suggest words to sum up the twentieth century, 'television', 'technology' and 'computer' were in the top ten, but so were 'holocaust' and 'genocide'. We humans seem intent on destroying each other. It is tragic. Something within tells us: *'It shouldn't be like this.'* We are left asking the old question, *'What's gone wrong with our world?'*

This was the subject of a series of letters in a newspaper some years ago. The best answer was also the shortest. It simply said: 'Dear Sir, What is wrong with the world? I am.' If we are honest with ourselves, we have to agree. We are the problem.

It was not always like this. To understand what went wrong we must consider the next great turning point in the history of the world, an event that is described in the third chapter of the Bible and is often called 'the Fall'.[4]

Adam and Eve are created to enjoy a perfect relationship with God in the Garden of Eden. He gives them just one

[4] See Genesis 3

command: they are not to eat from the tree of the knowledge of good and evil. But they both do just that and eat the fruit. It is an act of rebellion. God alone, as their Creator, has the right to decide how they should live, but Adam and Eve are not prepared to accept His authority. They take the crown off His head and place it firmly on their own, putting themselves in charge. 'From now on we will do things our own way,' they tell God.

This is not just ancient history. Adam and Eve stand for humanity as a whole. We would have done exactly the same if we had been there, and we repeat their sin every day of our lives. We are rebels against God. All the problems in our lives and in our world follow from that sin. The consequences of our disobedience are terrible. The perfect world that God made is spoilt. We no longer enjoy the peace that God intended. Instead we are at war with each other, the world we live in and – most seriously of all – with God. We resist His rule and, as a result, He is angry with us.

How does the Bible's account of the Fall end? With Adam and Eve being sent away from God's presence in the garden. To this day we remain cut off from God because of our refusal to submit to His loving rule over us. There is nothing we can do about it. Even if it was possible for us to live a perfect life from now on, we would still deserve God's punishment for our disobedience in the past. So where does that leave us? **Our only hope is if God takes the initiative to bring us back to Himself**. The wonderful news of the Bible is that He decided to do just that. From the very beginning He planned to put things right again.

The God who is there

> The comedian Spike Milligan was once asked: 'Do you ever pray?' He replied: *'Yes, of course, desperately, all the time: "Get me out of this mess." But I don't know who I am praying to.'*

Most people believe in some kind of god and even pray to him, but they have no idea of who this god really is. On our own, we will never be able to come to any certain knowledge about God. But what if He was to speak and tell us what He is like? Then we could know the truth. The Bible is a record of God doing just that.

A loving God

Since the Fall we have run away from God, but **in His great love He does not want to let us go**. The first part of the Bible (the Old Testament) describes how He began to implement His plan to call people back into friendship with Himself – a plan that was finally completed when Jesus came to earth. His actions tell us a great deal about the kind of God He is. The Bible is a revelation from God about Himself.

It all started with a promise. God appeared to Abraham, a man who lived near the Persian Gulf about four thousand years ago. God promised Abraham that He would reverse the effects of His judgement after the Fall. He would call a people back to Himself who could enjoy the benefits of His friendship once more. This people would at first be some of Abraham's descendants, the Israelites; but from the start, God made it clear that people from all over the world would be included. The Bible reveals how the promise was gradually fulfilled.

The Bible reveals how the promise was gradually fulfilled

A powerful God

There is only one God – the God who made the world. He has absolute power and continues to rule the world despite our rejection of Him. That power was seen by the people of Israel during the Old Testament period as they watched Him fulfil His promises to them. God looked after Abraham's descendants. When they became slaves in Egypt He acted to rescue them. All the firstborn sons of the Egyptians were killed in one night (known as 'The Passover') but God spared the Israelites and helped them to escape. The Egyptian army caught up with them at the Red Sea (the Sea of Reeds) so that they could pass through on dry land. When the Egyptians followed, the water returned and destroyed them. The Bible calls this great rescue 'The Exodus'.[5]

[5] See Exodus 12–13

He has absolute power **and continues to** rule the world despite our **rejection of Him**

A holy God

What do we mean by a holy God? **The 'holiness' of God is His complete perfection**. He loves what is good and hates what is evil. He wanted His people, the Israelites, to be holy like Him. So He gave them Laws to live by. These were revealed to the Israelites' leader, Moses, on Mount Sinai soon after the escape from Egypt. The main principles of God's Law were summed up in the Ten Commandments, in which God told the Israelites to put Him first in their lives and love each other.[6]

Soon after the giving of the Law, God gave the Israelites a land to live in. This was the Promised Land. Despite all that He had done for them, they did not obey God's Law. As the God of perfect justice He could not ignore their disobedience – He had to punish it. Although God was patient for a long time, He eventually acted in judgement. The Israelites were defeated by a foreign enemy, sent away from the land into exile and cut off from God's presence.

[6] Exodus 20:1-21

When England won the World Cup in 1966, Bobby Moore had the privilege of receiving the trophy from the Queen in front of the home crowd. Afterwards, he was asked what it had felt like.

'It was terrifying,' he replied. *'When I approached her I realized that the Queen was wearing some beautiful white gloves. I looked at my hands and they were covered in mud, and I thought "How*

can I shake hands with her like this? I will make her gloves dirty."'

If he was worried about approaching the Queen with his muddy hands, how much more should we be when we approach God? God does not just have white hands; He is perfectly clean all over. He is the holy God. And we don't just have dirty hands; we are dirty deep within because of what the Bible calls our 'sin' – we have disobeyed God's commandments. That is why the people of Israel were sent into exile away from His presence. So what hope is there for us?

The Old Testament ends with the promises of God unfulfilled. In His love God wants to have us as His friends, but how can that be possible? We are so imperfect and He is so holy. Justice demands that we are punished for our disobedience. God must find a way to be both loving and holy at the same time. From the start He had planned a solution, and He revealed it to His people through His spokesmen, the prophets. He would send a rescuer, or Saviour, 'the Christ'.

The down-to-earth God

Two thousand years ago, Jesus was born in Palestine alongside some animals in a stable – a humble start to life, though painters have since glamorized the scene. Mary always looks remarkably healthy for a woman who has just given birth; the baby Jesus has a gentle smile – even the straw looks as if it has been washed! The reality would have been rather different: dirty and smelly. **There was very little to suggest that this boy was anything out of the ordinary**. In one sense of course He was not – He was every bit as human as you or I. Yet the Bible's claim is that He was also divine: God Himself in human form – the down-to-earth God.

> Colonel James Irwin was one of the first men to walk on the moon. Soon afterwards he said: 'The greatest miracle is not that man stood on the moon. It is that God came and stood on earth.'

What do *you* make of Jesus? I had never thought seriously about Him until I was challenged to read one of the accounts of His life in the New Testament. I was amazed by what I discovered. Here was a man like no other.

The uniqueness of His claims

Jesus was a humble man but He made some extraordinarily self-centred claims. *'The time has come,'*

He said. *'The kingdom of God is near. Repent and believe the good news!'*[7] There is no doubt what He was saying. The prophets had predicted the coming of the kingdom of God – a time when God would enter His world, put everything right again and make it possible for people to know Him personally despite all they had done wrong.

Jesus was saying: *'The moment you have all been waiting for has arrived. I am the Christ of whom the prophets spoke, the one who will bring about the fulfilment of all God's loving promises.'*

Most religious leaders point away from themselves. 'Do you want to find God?' they ask, 'then go to that holy place' or 'read that holy book.' But Jesus said: *'I am the way the truth and the life. No-one comes to the Father except through me . . . Anyone who has seen me has seen the Father.'*[8] No one else has made such extraordinary claims. Jesus cannot be placed alongside Buddha, Mohammed and Confucius as just one religious teacher among many. He is unique.

The uniqueness of His life

Jesus' life supported His claims. Love poured out of Him – to young and old, male and female, rich and poor. He taught as no one else has ever taught. He had no formal education, but today millions of people are captivated by what He said and seek to live their lives according to His teaching. And He did astonishing miracles. He healed the lame, gave sight to the blind and raised the dead.

[7] Mark 1:15

[8] John 14:6 and 9. See also Matthew 11:28

The down-to-earth God

Jesus' life supported His claims. He was no lunatic suffering from self-delusion, no deceiver trying to make a name for Himself. He made extraordinary claims because He was an extraordinary man. He was who He said He was – the Son of God. He came to reverse the effects of the Fall and to restore our relationship with God. But how could He do that? It was not enough for Him to live on earth. He had to die.

Dying to meet you

One day in the early thirties AD, Jesus of Nazareth was arrested, put on trial, and sentenced to death by the Roman authorities. They nailed Him to a cross where He hung in agony for hours before He died. Crucifixion was one of the most terrible forms of execution ever devised. The Roman historian Cicero described it as 'a most vile and disgusting punishment.' We would expect the early Christians to be embarrassed by their founder's shameful death as a common criminal, but in fact they rejoiced in it. Jesus' death was at the centre of their message to others. Jesus Himself taught that He had to die. He could have avoided it, but He knew that it was necessary. Why? Why did Jesus have to die?

The Bible's answer is clear: **He died to satisfy God's love and justice**. We have seen that God is both loving and holy. Because of His love He longs to fulfil His promises, to bring people back into relationship with Himself. He wants us to enjoy His friendship but grieves for our rebellion against Him and cannot let this go unpunished.

How can such a friendship be made possible? Through the death of Jesus. In His great love God sacrificed His only son in our place. He did not deserve to die – He is the only person who has ever lived who has never done anything wrong – but on the cross He faced the punishment that we deserve. And the great result is that we can be friends with God again despite our disobedience.

Many years ago the Saxons and the Vikings were fighting in the north of Britain. They agreed to meet to discuss peace terms. There was one condition: no weapons could be brought. All obeyed except for one Viking, who hid a spear under his cloak and hurled it at the Saxon king as he approached. A Saxon lord called Liller saw the spear coming, and threw himself in front of it to shield his master. He died so that the king might live.

In a similar way Jesus died so that we might live. Peter, one of Jesus' closest friends, explained it like this: *'Christ died for sins once for all, the righteous for the unrighteous, to bring you to God.'*[9] We deserve the spear of God's anger for our disobedience, but instead, because of His great love, He sent His son Jesus to die for us. Jesus took our place on the cross, and died there instead. He willingly bore the full force of His Father's anger against our wrongdoing so that we wouldn't have to face it ourselves.

If we trust in Christ we can be sure that all our sin has been forgiven because Jesus took the punishment for it. We can be clean in God's sight. There is no other way by which we can be made right with Him. Do you really think

God would have sent His son to die if there was another way? We cannot get back to God by our own efforts. Our good works will never make us acceptable to Him. He is perfection and we are far from perfect. All of us – without exception – deserve to be separated from God forever, but because of the death of Jesus Christ we can be friends with Him no matter how bad we may have been. That is the wonderful news of Christianity.

Do you really think **God** would have sent His son to die **if there was another way?**

The day death died

How can we be sure that Jesus' death means that you and I can be friends with God today? The answer is, because of what took place two days later. **Jesus did not stay dead**. God raised Him to life again. And that is no myth; it actually happened. The resurrection is a fact of history for which there is compelling evidence. When Jesus' disciples went to the tomb on the first Easter Day they found that it was empty. Jesus had risen from the grave! He appeared to them on a number of occasions, talking and eating with them before ascending into heaven.[10] The disciples spent the rest of their lives proclaiming His resurrection to the world. It was a truth they were prepared to die for. Many of the early Christians were in fact killed for their faith.

How does the resurrection impact us? Some wonderful truths follow from the fact of the resurrection.

Jesus really is God's Son

He did not look like a mighty king as He hung in weakness on the cross, but that agonized man was and is the Lord of all. His friends buried Him in a tomb, but God raised Him to a throne. The resurrection reveals Jesus' true identity. It is God's great statement that Jesus truly is who He claimed to be – he was *'declared with power to be the Son of God, by his resurrection from the dead.'*[11] **Jesus' death really was successful. The cross was not an** accident, a tragic end to a promising young life. **It was meant to happen**. There was no other way by which God could forgive guilty people like you and me. And the resurrection shows that it worked. It proclaims God's approval of what His son did. He accepted Jesus' sacrifice of Himself as full payment of our debts.

Jesus really can be known today

I will never forget the words of some parents whose child had been killed in a road accident. They were devastated, but spoke movingly of how Jesus had been very close to them in their grief and helped them through. Until then it had never occurred to me that Jesus could be known and make a difference to our lives. I had thought that Christianity was about religious services and trying to obey a set of rules. But these people spoke of something different – a relationship. **I decided then that it was time I looked into the Christian faith for myself and began to read one of the Gospels**. As I did so, I found myself being drawn very strongly to the person of Jesus. He spoke to me not as a voice from the dead but as a living presence. **My life has never been the same since**.

Starting all over again

Have you experienced that awful moment in an exam when the teacher has just announced that there are only five minutes left? It is then that you suddenly realize you have completely missed the point of the first two questions. You want to tear up your paper and start again, but it is too late; there is no time left. We all feel like that sometimes with life. We have made mistakes. If only we could start all over again! We cannot turn back the clock, but we can make a fresh start. Wonderfully, God has made it possible. He offers a new beginning to all who trust in Christ.

Jesus' death and resurrection two thousand years ago made a new start possible. By His Spirit at work today what He achieved then may be effected in our lives now. The sending of the Spirit on the day of Pentecost is the next turning point in the history of the world.

[12] Acts 2:1-41

The book of Acts in the New Testament describes what happened.[12] The followers of Jesus were gathered together. There was a sudden loud noise and tongues of fire appeared to separate and come down on each of them. They began to speak in foreign languages that they had never spoken before. Peter explained what was happening. God was fulfilling one of the great promises He had made in the Old Testament – He was sending His Spirit to enter the lives of all His people.

There is only one God but He has revealed Himself to us in three persons: He is Father, Son and Holy Spirit. Since the day of Pentecost God the Spirit has been at work in all those who trust in Jesus.

What does the Holy Spirit do?

THE HOLY SPIRIT BRINGS NEW LIFE. The Bible teaches that we are spiritually dead because of our rebellion against God. We are quite helpless. It is no use going up to a dead body and shouting 'Come on, get up!' Dead people cannot do anything to help themselves. Spiritually we cannot do anything to help ourselves. It would take a miracle for 'dead' people like us to become spiritually alive to God. The Holy Spirit has been sent by God to make that miracle possible. As the good news about Jesus is explained, He opens people's eyes to understand the truth and then helps them to believe it.

HE GIVES POWER TO CHANGE. John had been thinking about the Christian faith for a while and had become convinced that it was true, but he could not commit to following Christ. There were so many things in his life that would not please Jesus. He felt he would never be able to change. 'It's no use,' he said as he sat in my study, 'I could never keep going.' He was quite right. On our own we will never be able to live the Christian life. The great news is that we are not on our own. As soon as we put our trust in Christ, the Holy Spirit enters our lives.[13]

[13] Romans 8:9; 1 Corinthians 12:13

He gives us a new desire to please God and a new strength to begin to put that desire into practice. We will not be perfect until we are in heaven, but the Spirit gives us the power to start to become more like Jesus.

HE EQUIPS GOD'S PEOPLE TO SERVE HIM. Jesus has given a job to all His followers – to tell the world about Him. Millions of people in countries across the world have never heard the name of Jesus. Many of our own families, friends and neighbours do not understand why He came to earth. We have a huge task. Though we are very weak, God has not left us to do the job on our own. The Holy Spirit helps us to tell others about Jesus.[14] This explains how it is that the Christian church has been able to grow so dramatically. The tiny group of believers in Jerusalem on the day of Pentecost has now become a great crowd of millions of people from every country throughout the world. All of them have been enabled by the Holy Spirit to start again with new life, a new power and a new job.

[14] Acts 1:8

Though we are very weak, **God has not left us** to do the job on our own

The end and the beginning

Missing The Point?

After the American troops were forced to surrender the Philippines to the Japanese in May 1942, General MacArthur vowed to retake the islands. He printed the words 'I will return' on thousands of leaflets which were then scattered across the country by aeroplanes. He kept his promise two years later.

Jesus made His intention to return to earth clear. Although the date of His coming is a secret, He taught on many occasions that we should not doubt that it will happen. The second coming of Jesus Christ will be the next great turning point in the history of the world. Jesus taught that when He comes, everyone who has ever lived will have to stand before Him and be judged.[15] There will be a great division. Some people will go to heaven, others will go to hell.

Hell

A few years ago sharks had been getting too close to the shore off some beaches in Australia. The authorities put up notices: 'Beware of the sharks!' Underneath was a picture of a fierce shark with vicious teeth. One mother complained that the signs were scaring her children. She had missed the point: these notices were meant to be frightening.

Jesus' teaching about hell was designed to have the same effect. He was the most loving man who has ever lived, but His teaching is full of references to hell. He took no pleasure in speaking of it; He did so only out of love. He wanted to warn people about a terrible reality. If we continue to choose to live our lives in rejection of God, in the end He will confirm that choice for ever. Hell is eternal separation from God, the source of all that is good in the world.

Hell is what we deserve. But because of Jesus' death, those who trust in Him can look forward to a very different future: heaven. That hope is certain for Christian believers; not because of anything we have done, but because of what Christ has done for us.

Heaven

When Jesus returns He will put everything right. He will bring this present fallen world to an end and introduce a new one. All the things that spoil life on earth will be removed. **There will be no sin, no sickness, no suffering, no sadness**. Instead there will be a new creation which will last for ever. It will be a perfect physical world with God at the centre.[16] At the moment we can only know God in part, but then we will see Him face to face. What a marvellous thought that is! No wonder the Bible ends with a prayer: *'Come, Lord Jesus.'*[17] Life will not be easy for those who try to follow Christ in a world that has rejected Him, but the certainty of a glorious future should inspire us to keep going.

[16] See Revelation 21:22 – 22:5   [17] Revelation 22:20

Turning point

The time has come for us to think about where we fit into the history of the world as it is presented in the Bible. We have seen that it is not a random process going nowhere. This world had a definite beginning and will have a definite end. God made everything and one day, when Christ returns, He will bring it to a close. But that will not be the end of history. It will be the beginning of a new creation, unspoilt and everlasting. God is delaying Christ's return so that more people might be ready for that great day. If we put our trust in Him, we need not fear hell but instead can have a certain hope of heaven.

What should I do?

We make many important decisions in our lives, such as who we will marry and what job we will do, but none is more important than how we choose to respond to Jesus Christ. Our eternal destiny depends on this choice. Jesus tells us what we should do. He said: *'Repent and believe the good news!'*[18]

REPENT

To repent means to turn around; it involves changing direction. We are called to completely re-orientate our lives, no longer living for ourselves alone, but recognizing the fact that Jesus is King. We are to live for Him. We are

[18] Mark 1:15

to take the crown from our head and hand it to Him, where it rightly belongs. That will involve saying sorry for the ways in which we have disobeyed Him and deciding from now on to follow His way through life. It will not be easy; there will have to be many changes. Our family and friends may not approve. But we are not on our own; God promises to send His Holy Spirit to all who turn to Christ.

BELIEVE

As those who have rebelled against God, we are in a serious situation, cut off from God and facing His judgement. There is nothing we can do about that; we are helpless and need rescuing. The good news is that Jesus came to earth to do that. By His death He did everything necessary to make it possible for us to be forgiven by God and accepted by Him forever. All we have to do is believe in Him, recognizing that without Him we have no hope of being friends with God.

Are you ready to make that choice? If so, you may find it helpful to use this prayer and make it your own:

Lord God, my Creator, I know that I have not put you first in my life. I do not deserve anything from you except your anger. But now I repent. I do not want to live for myself any more; I want to serve Jesus as my Lord. I thank you for sending Him to die on the cross in my place. I believe and trust that He died for me. Please come into my life by your Holy Spirit so that I might live for Jesus on earth, and be with Him forever in heaven. Amen.

If you have trusted in Christ you have experienced the most important turning point in your life. It may not feel very different at first. Trust in God's promises rather than your feelings. Jesus said: *'Whoever comes to me I will never drive away.'*[19]

What happens next?

If you have begun to follow Christ you will want to know what happens next. You have started a new life and you need help. Perhaps the best thing you can do to start with is tell someone – a Christian friend, someone who can help you along the Christian way. There is much to learn. In the Christian life you have:

A new Father

Because Jesus died for us, God has forgiven us for all that we have done wrong. Even the wrong things we will do in the future have been dealt with. We have been completely accepted by God and can now know Him as our heavenly Father. That is an amazing privilege. The Bible says: *'See how much the Father has loved us! His love is so great that we are called God's children!'*[20]

All relationships depend on speaking and being together, and that is also true of our friendship with God. We need to keep in touch with Him if we want it to grow. God speaks to us when we read the Bible and we can speak to Him through prayer. We can pray wherever we are, at any time. Many Christians have also found it helpful to

[19] John 6:37   [20] 1 John 3:1 (Good News Bible)

have a regular time to read a part of the Bible (the Gospels are a good place to start) and respond to God in prayer.

A new enemy

We have a new enemy when we start to follow Christ: the devil. He will do all he can to try to put us off course. He is strong, but we need not fear him. We could never resist the devil's power by ourselves, but God will help us if we look to Him.[21] Christ defeated the devil when He died on the cross, and He has given us His Spirit so that we can resist him.

A new companion

The Holy Spirit enters the lives of all those who trust in Christ. We do not see Him, but His presence is real. He will help us turn from what is wrong in our lives so that we can start going God's way. There will be things that you will need to repent of right away. Ask the Spirit to give you the strength to do that.

A new family

When God calls us to be His children we become, at the same time, brothers and sisters to all His other children: we belong to a new family. It is important that you find a local church to join, where the Bible is taught and the good news about Jesus is explained. You will find that the support of other believers is vital and you will be able to help them too.

[21] 1 Peter 5:8-9; 1 John 4:4

The Bible teaches that all those who belong to Christ should be baptized.[22] Baptism is the symbol that marks us out as followers of Christ. Talk to a minister at your church about this; they will be able to explain more about what this involves.

A new job

When He left the earth, Jesus gave His followers a job to do before He returned: to take the good news about Him into all the world. Is there someone you could tell? If that sounds frightening, be encouraged by the words of Jesus: *'Surely I am with you always, to the very end of the age.'*[23] We do not know when He will return. In the meantime it will often be hard to follow Him, but we can be sure of the presence of Christ by His Holy Spirit strengthening us and leading us on.

[22] Acts 2:38   [23] See Matthew 28:18–20

We can be sure of the presence of Christ by His Holy Spirit strengthening us and leading us on

Further information

If you would like more information about how you can
become a Christian, or would like help on living your new
life as a Christian, you can write to the Series Editor at
the address below. We would love to hear from you.

Exploring Christianity
c/o Authentic Media
9 Holdom Avenue
Bletchley
Milton Keynes
MK1 1QR

Further reading

A Fresh Start, J.C. Chapman (Matthias Media, 1997, reprinted; distributed by The Good Book Company)

Answers to Tough Questions, Josh McDowell and Don Stewart (Milton Keynes: Authentic Media, 2006)

Christianity Explored, Rico Tice and Barry Cooper (Surrey: The Good Book Company, 2005)

Real Lives, D.J. Carswell (Milton Keynes: Authentic Media, 2004, reprinted)

Turning Points, Vaughan Roberts (Milton Keynes: Authentic Media, 2006, reprinted)

Uncovered, Jonathan Carswell (Milton Keynes: Authentic Media, 2006, reprinted)

Uncovering the World, Jonathan Carswell (Milton Keynes: Authentic Media, 2006)

Why Believe? Roger Carswell (Milton Keynes: Authentic Media, 2004, reprinted)

Why Should God Bother with Me? Simon Austen (Tain: Christian Focus, 2002)

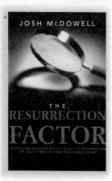

Distinctives
by Vaughan Roberts

Daring to be different in a different world

In a fresh and readable style Vaughan Roberts issues a challenging call to Christians to live out their faith. We should be different from the world around us – Christian distinctives should set us apart in how we live, think, act and speak.

Targetting difficult but crucial areas such as our attitude to money and possessions, sexuality, contentment, relativism and service, this is holiness in the tradition of J.C. Ryle for the contemporary generation. Roberts helps us to consider how we are to respond biblically to the temptations and pitfalls surrounding us – giving what we cannot keep, to gain what we cannot lose.

Will you take up the challenge?

Will you dare to be different?

ISBN: 978-185078-331-2

*Available on **www.authenticmedia.co.uk**
or from your local Christian bookshop*

Real Lives
by D.J. Carswell

'You are on a train; you look at the people around you. Someone hides behind a newspaper. Another dozes; a young man nods to the beat from his iPod. A baby cries further along the carriage and a table of football fans celebrate an away victory over a few cans of lager. Someone's mobile goes off; a student sitting next to you sends a text message. Eavesdropping on the conversations, you catch soundbites from those around you. Who exactly are they, you wonder?'

> *Real people*
>
> > *All different*
> >
> > > *Everyone with a life story*
>
> *Real lives*

In *Real Lives* you will meet, among others . . . a famous footballer . . . a sophisticated lady from South Africa . . . an Olympic athlete . . . a backpacker exploring the States . . . a Brahmin from India . . . a young, abused girl . . . the greatest man in history who was a child refugee . . . and the author's own story of a changed life.

ISBN: 978-185078-412-8

*Available on **www.authenticmedia.co.uk**
or from your local Christian bookshop*